I0223899

At The End of My Bones

poems by

Naomi Leimsider

Finishing Line Press
Georgetown, Kentucky

At The End of My Bones

Copyright © 2026 by Naomi Leimsider
ISBN 979-8-89990-322-9 First Edition
All rights reserved under International and Pan-American Copyright Conventions.
No part of this book may be reproduced in any manner whatsoever without written
permission from the publisher, except in the case of brief quotations embodied in
critical articles and reviews.

ACKNOWLEDGMENTS

Thank you to the editors of the following journals where these poems first
appeared:

Unleash Lit, "Cauda Equina", "Scare"
Heavy Feather Review, "Middle Pain"
Mantis, "Patient Is Now Unable at Multiple Levels (Notes)"
Midway Journal, "Already the Decline"
Lothlorien Poetry Journal, "Madness", "Bad Nights"
Ellipsis, "Soft Bones"
Branches, "On the Game Show"
Mid-Atlantic Review, "Section/Grave/Block, Flushing, NY," "At the End of
My Bones

Publisher: Leah Huete de Maines
Editor: Christen Kincaid
Cover Art: Naomi Leimsider
Author Photo: Naomi Leimsider
Cover Design: Elizabeth Maines McCleavy

Order online: www.finishinglinepress.com
also available on amazon.com

Author inquiries and mail orders:
Finishing Line Press
PO Box 1626
Georgetown, Kentucky 40324
USA

Contents

This book is dedicated to my wonderful dad
Richard Jay Leimsider
April 29th, 1946 – February 3rd, 2024

And to my amazing mom
Lydia Leimsider

And to my outstanding Zoë
and my fantastic Joel
"You are the loves of my life and my whole heart"

"Tell me, what else should I have done?
Doesn't everything die at last, and too soon?
Tell me, what is it you plan to do
with your one wild and precious life?"

The Summer Day
Mary Oliver

"I met a traveller from an antique land
Who said: "Two vast and trunkless legs of stone
Stand in the desert . . . Near them, on the sand,
Half sunk, a shattered visage lies, whose frown,
And wrinkled lip, and sneer of cold command,
Tell that its sculptor well those passions read
Which yet survive, stamped on these lifeless things,
The hand that mocked them, and the heart that fed:
And on the pedestal these words appear:
'My name is Ozymandias, king of kings:
Look on my works, ye Mighty, and despair!'
Nothing beside remains. Round the decay
Of that colossal wreck, boundless and bare
The lone and level sands stretch far away."

Ozymandias
Percy Bysshe Shelley

Middle Pain

Up against the faceless ghost clock
again. Time is of the essence.
Waiting for the one-sided
middle pinch,
that sets it all in motion.
Cycle in. Cycle out. So, so smooth the way it
sheds and grows.
How it all goes.

The inner mechanism slows and shifts.
Only able to harness stillness,
can't control its absence,
so run like the devil across to the median strip,
that narrow no man's land divided down the middle,
and make a late-century phone call
in a mid-century phone booth
in the middle of the concrete island
in the middle of a highway.

Phone calls cost a quarter. Put the coin in
and make the call.
Make the call in the phone booth
in the middle of the land in between.
In the place that goes in
different directions.
Where decisions don't have to be made.
Where you don't
have to ask permission.
In the middle of the highway,
in the phone booth,
do what needs to be done.
Waiting for the one-sided middle pain
that won't come.

The silent ghost clock tracks time,
and the race against its absence.
The middle pain of being neither here nor there
or anywhere really.
Not being able to find the way, get it all going,
get the ball rolling
again, so run like the devil and find the phone booth
in the middle place,
in the middle of aching,
in the middle of the highway.
Make the call. Do what needs to be done.
Count time: all the seconds, minutes,
as they go by.

Up against the eternal ghost clock
again. The way it is shrouded, deceptive.
The way it should spin clockwise
back and forth
back and forth
but not this time.

In the middle of things.
What needs to be done.
Cycle in. Cycle out.
Midway, it always shoots through,
so run to the middle
of the concrete island,
in the middle of the highway,
make a late-century phone call
in the mid-century phone booth.
The landscape, the grid, the clock.
Faceless, still: time itself.
Make the call.
Do what needs to be done.
Waiting for the one-sided middle pain
that won't come.

Scare

Once, in a twilight sleep so deep it was just shy of a fugue state, I
set forth on a fact-finding mission following the curving path of my
hijacked mind.
Back on the straight line, still shimmering around the edges,
were the occasional sparks and shocks of distant cramps, phantom
pains, fleeting discomfort,
start-and-stop symptoms, but, in time, they—
and the remnants of reality—ceased to exist, so in the stark face of
grim discoveries that require grim decisions,
I gave into the dark energy in that new realm. There are always
thresholds to cross.

I want to tell you what I saw there. Show you all the sights there were
to behold. As you might imagine,
everything requires surgical extraction.
When you are not awake yet awake, they cut out organs,
inspect them for margins.
In the soft, glowing light of this
particular purgatory, your body parts are up for examination.

Smallish feet smoothly separated—somehow—from their long-ago
child legs, once burned,
then bloodless, dry, without juice or mucus
or oils and stripped down to gray-brown bones were on display.
A pair of previously ashy, dirty lungs busily repairing themselves in real
time before the damage couldn't be undone.
Everything on a tight schedule. Spines twisting—some with
potential trouble—in primordial bodies,
bobbing in great glass tanks: which one, which one, would I choose?
What was once a rough patch of rigid removed skin biopsied within
an inch of itself
—dug so deep, stretched so tight—that only flimsy wrinkled
tissue remained. Thousands and thousands of abandoned, neglected
eggs, jellied and slick,
swimming in their own wet universe, popping with
possibility one at a time, then dying all at once on the vine. Thickened
veins stood out against the tangible parts of the pulsing organ in

question. The distance, the space—negative but tactile—between what I didn't know
and what I would soon learn. Once, before this, I bit a finger on
my essential left hand—hard to the bone but did not lop it off—
and for the first time understood the power of the body in parts.
The bite force of a mammal's mouth. The want, the fear, the intent of hunger.
It will eat you alive.

I can't promise they won't feed whatever is left, the scraps, piecemeal,
from your physical form, —still bloody, still beating—to the local
wildlife, to the animals living on the edge of existence. It's okay. We all
need to be fed. What is left except to have bits and pieces removed,
and wonder what to do with the leftovers. Wander in the dark long enough, dream when you
are not supposed to dream, and you
might find yourself compelled to take that desperate drag of pure
oxygen, prep for colorless camouflage, slip into an exoskeleton,
just in case there are sudden shudders, whispers, calling you back,
as they called me, and for once, I thought, I listened.

Maybe I never left. All memory is temporary, so how did they put
me back together? How we acknowledge what can happen, the precariousness
of how we slip out and slip in. How to accept the violent injury of
realizing that one chapter
has ended, and another will soon begin.

Soft Bones

Nothing shakes my soft addiction
to my soft bones.
This condition, this soft situation,
some say, is nothing:
I can bend and bend
and bend but won't break.
Some say maybe
I'm a corner case. But I'm

full of holes. From flank to hips
to ribs on both sides: all those bones.
Maybe the spaces in my skull
never closed.
Sudden sounds:
acid growls, gurgling.
Feeling all the visceral
things. Deficient and clearly
tweaking. In and out of these

soft compulsions, but maybe I
should clean myself up
and look nice now, nothing like my
current condition.
Cover my bones in
a new soft sweater.
Brighten my face with
a feather light swipe.
Fix my thick hair with
hard metal pins. Let cuticle skin
grow out and around
gnawed nails so short

and sharp. I don't smoke or drink
anymore,
still I am told
maybe just
inhale, take a shot or two,

swallow a few
little pills,
get some soft
dreamless sleep.

But no, I can't!
What about my tender bones?
I have these tender bones!
My own meat falls off
my own bones are so soft.
Long ago, they promised to be strong,
hold me up. Maybe I ignored
all the signs, tip-offs,
along the way: slipping hips, slipped discs,
slipping ribs. So seductive
those numb spots, clicking jaw, fuzzy
fingers and toes. I've been told:

Don't be frightened; it is all normal.
But I am
suddenly
so easy to mold,
so full of soft addictions, and I make excuses,
so many excuses—it's quite the situation—
so strung out
so catch me cornered
so far from recovered.
I will not give it up; I hold it close.
The body is so greedy, and
I am at the end of my bones.

Cauda Equina

At the long end of the lumbar line, listen for the wild rumors,
whispers of warnings: collapse is coming.
In the beginning, there was violence, too.
Fresh nerve explosions, the beat-to-beat regimented repetition
of the segmentation clock, then each knob, root, and ring stacking
one on top of the other,
a bundle of shock absorbers, coiled springs, begets the graceful

curves of five sections from cervical top to horse's tail. Thirty-three
prehistoric bones grow, fuse, take up more and more room
in their own small universe.
Years and years later, the rising chatter reveals those same nerves
frayed like fried wires, scorched beyond repair,
pressed into less and less space.
Gradual onset gives way to the full pull of gravity. One last sound:
the deep

groan of devastated molecules, particles—separating, rearranging—
before being thrust into this yawning abyss.
Down and down and down.
Then silence.
Stunted and stilled at the bottom of the world. Above you,
the atmosphere thins:
it is hard to believe they expect you to breathe. What else do they
want you to do?
Get up; walk it off? Remember walking around. Footsteps
upstairs. The feel

of feet on the ground. Delicate lungs can regenerate, repair. The liver
grows its own tissue, too.
Skin hardens, scars. But the spine—oh, the
spine!—does it
dirty. What's done is done. What's lost is lost. No one denies the night
is long. That there will be more violence.
It is sensible for you to remain inflamed, nauseous, stunned.
Someone needs to tick off time while you wait for those
thirty-three

bones—calcium hard, collagen spongy—to succumb. Someone needs
to bear witness to the ones
that bend, compress, into other dimensions.
They used to call it
shellshock when there would be no more messages received,
nothing here or there,
no more sensation, but you can still send signals into space,
shrug off form and function.
Don't look down; it is too late for questions.

Already the Decline

In real life, I put my head in a machine. How is this brain different
from all other brains?
My transient, shifting butterfly-shape of a landscape in its final
stage—possibly shrinking,

almost definitely frayed—but already on the downswing. Wired into
the surface, the metallic
clatter of pulsing attachments, steel stimulation, determines levels of
insult. Pay the pons toll,

cross from midline to stem, and report back news from the far away
fore. No more secrets.
No more hiding. I am the system, and the system is me. Only the
malignant promises of

incidental findings: old scars abutting new formations; ripe berry
cysts that might burst and
bleed black, red, and blue all over the floor; dotted maps of mild
white matter pointing wildly

in different directions; little ruptures revealed in the deepest recesses
below the grey surface.
How do all other brains survive the interminable wait for silence? The
incessant clacking,

rattling, droning disappears me one click at a time in this heavy metal
world within the
world within the world. I already know what is already happening:
the vanishing of years and years

and years of carefully curated thoughts, collected ideas, vivid visions.
Does the brain know
what is within it is real? I thought I was just getting started and
already the decline.

Madness

It is not the good kind, but it's also not what you think it is.
You think.
Growing without influence in its own environment, it can be quite
overstimulated and hyperactive.
If it flares up again, you might not make it out.
Chip away
at its organic state created from mutations and mistakes and out of
control manifestations.

Does it have its own beating heart?
How will you know? And when you know,
will there finally be silence and peace
in the knowing?

When it shows itself, it is coarse-haired, jagged, snaggled. Knotted up
on top and unseeing.
A chipped tooth, one of two, jutting out
of the wrong place.
What a faceless face! This is one of those that grows hair and teeth
and maybe mirrors
the way you will look in the future. Look at it: see your
future self.

Will there be more to come?
It senses you have succumbed, contorted like you are
in your wild shape. You were so close
this time. It wants you to know you almost made it out.

Patient is Now Unable at Multiple Levels
(Notes)

Patient is a person who experienced sudden onset consistent with
evidence. History
has been severe—very severe— the present is what it seems, and the
future, as always,
is unknown, undetermined. This situation—and perhaps others to
come—notwithstanding.

Some function, little function, waning function, absence of function
(incomplete may become complete or remain)

After long days of nothing who can say.
How to communicate this: You will now
live in the small space between.

How to explain?

    First there was bled out fluid—it trickled, gushed,
reabsorbed, trickled
    again—through the slow flow of malformations in barely
visible caverns.

    Imagine a vessel traveling through the tangle of bloody
networks down
    expanding paths among lost soft lesions in such spacious
places, in immense
    dark depths, only to find it abandoned, hollowed out, in
rapid decline.

    Consider a come and go violent injury without violence, a
cavernous
    complex formation followed quickly by degeneration. A
complicated
    incomplete yet complete non-injury injury. Hemorrhagic and
sporadic.

You are in need of acute awareness: the divide in
understanding is,
        quite clearly, deep and wide.

Extensive evaluation then prepped with no clear reason
(difficulty obtaining clearance). Struck down by slowness,
out of the bare minimum of luck. Patient introduced to the useless
universe, the long reach
of time. Did time forget what to do, how to move?

        Patient is now unable at multiple levels.

Remember the old adage: A pumped stomach always reveals its
contents.
Ask Patient: how do you feel?
Ask Patient: how do you hurt?
Ask Patient: who are you now?

Evidence is extensive, so extensive, but still
we ask: Same, worse, or better? Same, worse, or better?
For more significant revelations ask
specific questions!
But in the end, we rely on summary again and again:
Delicate surgery begets no surgery;
difficult clearance begets no clearance.
Evaluate and evaluate and evaluate,
but do not encourage.
Reassess, reassess, reassess,
then do not bother.
Patient is
unable.
Unable to seek
care
Unable to facilitate
care

Unable to know
who will
care,
do the
caring,
how to
care.

Do Not Share:
Perhaps you have arrived at the last place. Do not think
about other possibilities. You wondered where or when
or how it would come: the time is now. Do not consent:
it shouldn't have happened this way, but you borrowed
time. Hijacked, ransacked, plundered time until the moment,
the very last moment, before unexpected event. Do not
consult: what more could anyone say. What can and
cannot, will and will not, happen next is never known.
Do not consider: none of us can enhance or assess or
reason with chance. Did you listen for the ringing, the
warning shot: you are out of time. This is it. Now. This
is what will take you down.

Bad Nights

I am my own doomsday clock. It's disruptive when some say I'm a smart girl
and a smart girl should be able to avoid this level of conflict, of catastrophe,
at every turn. What I did when I was told what to do; all will be well if only I
could follow the rules. Now it's late, and, as usual, I don't understand the assignment.

And there are things I should have done when I was on the very edge of annihilation,
waiting for the big threat to pass. It might be after the war, but I am still in the fog
looking for clear paths. When does my tour end so I can go home, turn it back. After all,
time is only a way of ticking past.

And if there is ever another morning, I will eat rationed butter pats on baskets of bread,
big bites of salty powdered eggs, also ersatz cream whipped with replacement oil
in strong bulletproof coffee. If I still like anything, I like to be under incredible duress,
then earn my small pleasures—be truly good and hungry—before I fill up to a full belly.

And a smart girl would know better than to exist as a terrible risk to all, I know. I should
be beyond full-scale plans, situation maps, a serious getting into it, with no reason for
anyone to panic. Whatever happens now will be a symbol of how I'm never quite sure
what to examine, how to comprehend the given guidelines, the go ahead, follow directions.

But I'm a smart girl—so it goes—and there are things I should know.
I still keep this
weapon tucked under my well-worn wings, in the waning minerals of
my ribs, where the real
danger lives. What I do know is all possible futures have been
knocked down to the last:
we can't take the world with us when we go. And I just want to take it
with me when I go.

Section/Grave/Block, Flushing NY

"Charon, the ferryman of the dead, his hand on the boat-pole, calls me now: 'Why are you tarrying? Make haste, you hinder my going!' He speaks impatiently, urging me on with these words."
Alcestis (255), Euripides

Inside, your heart weakly beating, rigors rising, wounds weeping –
they are sad, too, overwhelmed, out of options – and you are
at the end of your bones.
Outside, it is late in the yellowed afternoon. Beyond windows and
walls, beyond buildings
and borders, in the gray misery of the river, is the skull-adorned
bony spine of the boat we all know. As your first-born, and now,
your guide down this
particular path, I am also out of options, with nowhere else to go.

I should have money to lend, extra funds of any kind. You suggested I
save, but I didn't
listen, so I have no coins for your journey. Let's not pay Charon
anyway!
We can just say we are lost and blame my bad map skills. Or proclaim
we are on the outs:
we won't join queues, follow his rules. Still, you seem resigned,
ready for the river, on your way to slip through. Don't give in to him!
Stay with us on this
side; don't make the grim choice to cross forever.

So let's not pay Charon! I don't mind being haunted if you don't mind
a hundred years
wandering around down and out on the riverbed. We love
purgatories, right?
So many cautionary tales come from crowded limbos: those
delicious, treacherous
spaces. Perhaps you met Charon before, were introduced, briefly,
so you know when it is your time to cross the river it won't include
me. Charon isn't confused
by my presence, he knows this is our first nodding acquaintance.

In the late afternoon, they come in and prepare you. In the late
afternoon, comes sullen Charon
in his precarious boat. Expecting his tip.
But I won't let him touch your bones. Would never let him touch
your bones.

If you get in, in there, in his makeshift boat, you will never be out
here, on the outside, again.

Please don't say you'll pay Charon! He's ugly and surly and nobody
likes him. Don't look at
him or meet his knowing gaze. Go no contact! I'll be all about
keeping Charon's chaos under control,
organize the future within an inch of our lives
because organization insists
on more time. If you get in, you will be beyond the realm of my
vision. If you get in,
he will whisk you away! And I know why you won't let
me dip in a testing toe
or two: I wasn't raised to be charming; I have nothing to barter
or trade.

In the late afternoon, comes churlish Charon in his flat, low boat.
You pull your eyes open,
so you can see me, one last time, keenly, bright, in the artificial light.
Sometimes night comes early. Soon it will be too dark to see. I am
here, outside, where I will
keep an eye on the world for you. Oh, but inside is my own heart,
my own organs, my own bones! For now, they are still ripe and
whole. You board the boat;
Charon has lost all patience, and it is time to go.

Is It Like Being Lost

because I know what that's like.
   When it's late,
and I walk the wrong way down the wrong street again.
   When I lay it down,
give it up, there and nowhere and here and disappear,
      where will I be?

I go looking for you, but I need a mind
    not like mine,
with its severe lack of cognitive maps, perception, regulations.
    I should be taken out
back, buried under street signs, way under the framework of the
    familiar yet unfamiliar
grid. When you don't know where you are, you lose your body.
      Three-dimensional patterns
appear flattened, the universe's rules upended. Upside down,
     trying to go back
the way I came, but always in the wrong direction.

People's ideas about how to fix the problem
    don't address what to do
with the bits and pieces, frayed fragments, of my brain's scattered
      debris. So little ability
to balance, calibrate distance, that one day I'll slide off the wrong side
    of the familiar yet unfamiliar
grid, on the wrong block, on the wrong street, in the wrong home.
    And then I won't live anywhere anymore.

You always knew where you were,
     where you were going,
but I still tell people you are lost as explanation. Did you know it
    instantly? I know the way
you can suddenly know you are not in the right place. Until now,
      you haven't known
what it's like to be counted among the missing, that other people's ideas
    about how to fix the problem

leave you abandoned, stranded, in the wrong spaces, calling in from
                              remote places,
where search parties can't locate any signs of life or be seen.

More often than not,
             it's late, and I am still somewhere,
but I can't see what's ahead of me. When you don't know
             where you are,
you lose your body. How will I let go, like you, transition from
             tethered to untethered
on this familiar yet unfamiliar grid. When I walk the wrong way
                              down the wrong street,
lay it down there and nowhere and here and disappear.
             When I give it up, where will I be?

On the game show,

like in life, the pretty girls go first, so you find yourself somewhere
down the line.
Stringing you along with so much at stake! How much will it take
to start again? All gigged up on cortisol, on chance. The anticipation
of all that you might win. Of what can be won.
This could be—finally—your time!
Maybe, maybe.
You sit in the back, eyes big and black with adrenaline, with bargains,
waiting
your turn. Your face will eventually be on the giant screen,
so follow the instructions on how and what to fix.
Various color wheel contour hacks, shades for all your sides
shortcuts, increase
or decrease your nose, mouth, chin twists.
The day moves. By the time you get to the front of the line,
you outgrow your former life.
One more dopamine pump and you shed your skin all in one go: you
have shaken off
your old self! You surrender to the pleasure
of being lost to promises.
Now you must answer the questions correctly! This is what you came
here to do.
This is what is expected of you.
What comes first, next, last? Basics, facts. Smart girls answer first,
but you
wander through the bleak, dismal world
of what you thought you knew. There is a chance you might actually
know some
of the answers—*maybe, maybe*—but they still want you to want
what they conjured just for you: free drinks, a thoughtfully catered
lunch, bags brimming
with consolations.
What can they do for you? What can they get you?
But you can't afford this, and what is borrowed needs to be returned.

How will you know if you
are a success? If you win

—maybe, maybe—
what will be your prize?
All this, all this.
                    Oh, the wanting!
The day ends at the beginning of an untangling. Maybe you got some of the answers
right, but it's not enough. It's never enough.
You already submitted to changing your face, so you could be up on that screen
for all to see. You sloughed off your old self,
left yourself behind. Your used body. Molted soft. Metabolism slowed.
Is this—are you—even real?
They cut you
loose. Push you
out. You have to go back to who you were before. Back to your life.
You have to go back to your life.

Sick Headache

The ache in your head is all in your head,
         even if it is sometimes in your stomach, but it is not
            a stomachache.
You feel it in your stomach, yes,
         but it is in your head even when it is not
            in your head.
The dizziness is either your ears or head, or neither ears nor head,
            but it is not in your stomach
               or because of your stomach.

The stomachache is the headache is the dizziness
                  is probably just your anger talking to you.
Your stomachache is the headache is the dizziness
               are just your feelings dying to be heard.
Find someone who will hear you, really hear you,
            with a solid pair of great big listening ears.

However, maybe you are sick, in fact, sick with something specific,
               so the recent giddiness is, perhaps,
                  a deep thumping near your brain stem,
                     or in that stomach place,
                        which is also what the musty metallic taste in
your mouth
               might be about, and, possibly, last year's bout of half-body
               numbness, various neurological insults, a last-minute
               case of the shakes, and the yips.

But if you insist, if you lean in hard, will they still drill medieval holes
                  to see how many humours they can release,
                     then use slick modern tools to remove your
ingrown horns,
                     mitigate your ancient desire for the bitter taste
of the blood
                     of others or drain you of yellowed sputum
                        and the many earthy colors of congestion?

After that, you probably won't be easily startled anymore.
  After that, your seemingly intractable issues may just go away.

Some of the greats suffered mightily in ways like these, but you, as
you know,
                    have nothing in common with them.
                    You are not as important as you were hoping
you might be.
                    You have not been a shining example of your
people.
                    You have done nothing to save or change
lives, so haul
yourself
                    over to the local emergency for a glucose
drip and a
scolding from
                    the doc: your aches are in your stomach
or your head
or your ears
                    or wherever.
You know you are not supposed to be able to feel the enamel peeling
       off your teeth,
                    or the microscopic goings on of unicellular
organisms
                    on the harsh, vast landscape of your skin.
Then there is the mysterious case of the five-day ache, and, again,
your stomach,
                    only this time on the other side,
                    or the way you have forgotten where to look,
                    how to gaze, where to put your eyes in useful places.

You haven't been yourself.
            You've really caught a case.
            You've been talking, recently, about being so far past the
middle of things,
            counting beats until the end, but still you are told all
you need,

all you need is just to be brave.
Now you'll have to go back the way you came.
Never mind the bargains and the bills to pay.
Someday, someone will ask: Why did you wait so
long?
Someday, you might find yourself paralyzed
in your last wild place,
and then, someday, it will be too late.

The Yips

I felt it go. Something released in me, and it was gone. Once released,
something moved in me, and it was gone. I've forgotten everything:
the unexplained mechanics of how to be in a body, the difficult
specifics of moves, decisions.
What is left is the bellwether buzzing of bone on
bone, the way old scars ache when they wake up, how nerve damage
dulls jagged edges.

This is the falling apart bit, untied as I am, unravelling,
strand by strand.
The interruption of basic functions can be temporary, but also might
mean they are gone for good.
What still exists is the somewhat dubious
promise that one day, once again, I will remember.
And that I can relearn what everything is for
and what it does and why. What falls apart can,
someday, be put back together.

Another Name

When you returned to your original existence, you were given
        another name.   I don't know you
    by that name.   Nobody has ever known you
    by that name.   To me, you still have the name I knew,
    but now you   are someone else.

You have become such and such or so and so, one of many
    standard stand-ins for names lost to the loss of muscle
memories. You are again son of your father, to whom you once
    belonged. The transition is not just slapping a new name
on an old face, but, still, I am supposed to just adjust to you being
    such and such or so and so, and son of your father once
again. It separates us the way we haven't been since long-ago,
    before I was born. My name is the last name we shared.

                Such strange jealousy.
    Which name should I say when I say your name now?
    Is the name that you gave me not my real name, too?
            I am still in the middle of things.
        All this naming and renaming, in the grand
    scheme of things, is the long game. As I wait to become,
        once again,   daughter of you.

At the End of My Bones

Who were these bones for if not for you.
Watch me and wait for the wearing away. Slim, long, thin
on the scan: hairline fractures everywhere.
You'll slice your fingers open following the patterns, so don't
trace my splits at the neck, the thighs, the hips.
Sharp points at the turned-up collar. Bonds broken between
bumps and bones. Shocks in back. Small breaks
in spaces. Sudden collapse. This won't end well. Neither
surgery nor medicine will fix this mess.

Who was this body for if not for you.
I wait my turn while you watch and wait for the wearing
away. Stay with me. Our uneasy relationship
with memory. Still, imagine us the way we were.
Everything in its place then. Pulling its own
weight then. Those whole dull-edged bones, covered top to
bottom with smooth skin. So soft, so lovely.
Watch and wait for what happens next and when. We won't
wait long for it to set in. Watch me wearing away.

Naomi Bess Leimsider's poetry book, *Wild Evolution*, was published by Cathexis Northwest Press in June 2023. She has published poems, flash fiction, and short stories in *Branches, Ellipsis, Lothlorien Poetry Journal, Midway Journal, Heavy Feather Review, Mantis, Unleash Lit, Packingtown Review, Tangled Locks Journal, The Avenue Journal, Booth, Anti-Heroin Chic, Wild Roof Journal, Planisphere Quarterly, Little Somethings Press, Syncopation Literary Journal, On the Seawall, St. Katherine Review, Exquisite Pandemic, Orca, Hamilton Stone Review, Rogue Agent Journal, Coffin Bell Journal, Hole in the Head Review, Newtown Literary, Otis Nebula, Quarterly West, The Adirondack Review, Summerset Review, Blood Lotus Journal, Pindeldyboz, 13 Warriors, Slow Trains, Zone 3, Drunkenboat,* and *The Brooklyn Review.*

In addition, she has been a finalist for the Acacia Fiction Prize, the Saguaro Poetry Prize, and the Tiny Fork Chapbook Contest. In 2022, she received a Pushcart Prize nomination for fiction. She teaches creative writing and expository writing at Hunter College/CUNY.

www.ingramcontent.com/pod-product-compliance
Lightning Source LLC
Chambersburg PA
CBHW022051080426
42734CB00009B/1292